FRANKLIN D. ROOSEVELT

From the New Deal
to the Second World War

Written by Thomas Melchers
Translated by Rebecca Neal

History 50MINUTES.com

FRANKLIN D. ROOSEVELT

KEY INFORMATION

- **Born:** 30 January 1882 in Hyde Park (New York).
- **Died:** 12 April 1945 in Warm Springs (Georgia).
- **Political party:** Democratic Party.
- **Election dates:**
  - 8 November 1932;
  - 3 November 1936;
  - 5 November 1940;
  - 7 November 1944.
- **Time in office:** 12 years.
- **Main achievements:**
  - The New Deal in response to the Great Depression.
  - The USA's entry into the Second World War on the Allied side.

INTRODUCTION

Franklin D. Roosevelt is the only president of the USA to have been elected for four consecutive terms, and now ranks alongside George Washington (1732-1799) and Abraham Lincoln (1809-1865) as one of the country's most famous and revered presidents.

He was born in 1882, was a member of the Democratic Party, and played a crucial role on the national and international stage in the 1930s and 1940s. He began his political career as governor of the state of New York, but his reputation rests on his actions as president. He was first elected three years after the 1929 Wall Street Crash, which plunged the USA into the Great Depression, and implemented the New Deal, an interventionist programme which revived the country's economy. He is also remembered for bringing the USA's isolationist policy to an end following the Japanese attack on the Pearl Harbor naval base in December 1941. After bringing his country into the war, Roosevelt, as commander-in-chief of the US army, played a central role in the Allied victory. At the end of the war he attended the Yalta Conference (February 1945) and laid the foundations for the United Nations.

After he contracted polio in the 1920s, Roosevelt's lower limbs were left paralysed. He retired from the presidency in March 1945 due to his declining health, and died of a massive brain haemorrhage at his home in Georgia on 12 April. His death sent shockwaves across the US and around the world. As stipulated in the United States Constitution, it was left to his vice-president, Harry S. Truman (1884-1972), to serve the remaining three years of his term and put an end to the war.

BIOGRAPHY

A PRIVILEGED UPBRINGING

Franklin Delano Roosevelt was born on 30 January 1882 to a wealthy aristocratic family. His father, James Roosevelt (1928-1900), was descended from Dutch immigrants who arrived in America in the 17th century, while his mother, Sara Ann Delano (1854-1941), whose family had also immigrated during that era, had Franco-Luxembourgish roots. Thanks to his mother's business interests, in particular in the opium trade with China, the future president inherited a vast fortune.

The young Franklin spend his childhood in the countryside at Hyde Park, around 60 miles from New York City, and abroad, particularly in Europe, where he learnt French and German. After being home-schooled as a child, from the age of 14 he attended the prestigious Groton School in Massachusetts, which emphasised the values of Christian duty, charity and patriotism. He enrolled at Harvard in 1889 to study for his

BA, then continued his studies at Columbia University Law School, but lacked interest and soon dropped out.

| Photograph of Roosevelt at Groton School at the age of 18.

EARLY POLITICAL CAREER

Roosevelt's career began in 1907 when, having passed the bar exam in New York, he started working for a prestigious law firm on Wall Street to contribute towards his family's expenses. However, he had little enthusiasm for his work.

Roosevelt had briefly met his distant cousin Eleanor Roosevelt (1884-1962) as a child, but met her again at a society event in New York in 1902. They saw each other on a number of occasions that year. Eleanor was the niece of Theodore Roosevelt and, like her uncle, was descended from the branch of the family that came from Oyster Bay, while Franklin belonged to the other branch, which originated from Hyde Park. Their shared ancestor was Nicholas Roosevelt (1658-1742), the son of the first Roosevelt to arrive in the New World.

Eleanor was orphaned before the age of 10 and educated at a prestigious English boarding school. While there, she developed a passion for current events, learnt French and travelled around the continent. She met Franklin shortly after her return to the USA. They were married on 17 March 1905, with Theodore Roosevelt as one of their wedding guests, and went on to have six children together, one of whom died in infancy.

His career turned in a new direction in 1910, when the Democratic Party, which saw him as the ideal candidate due to his prestigious family name and immense fortune, approached him about entering politics. After a somewhat unconventional campaign, he was elected senator for the state of New York in 1911. During his term, he fought against corruption within the Democratic Party and attracted the attention of Woodrow Wilson (1856-1924), the recently elected Democratic president.

From the navy to the vice-presidential candidacy

In March 1912, Roosevelt stepped down as senator to follow Wilson to Washington D.C., where he became assistant secretary of the navy

(1913-1921). He was passionate about everything related to navigation and threw himself into his new role, taking an interest in both national and international issues, although he did not share the pacifistic views of Wilson's government when the First World War broke out in 1914. As part of this role, he was sent to the front to inspect the US naval forces, where he met Winston Churchill (1874-1965), who at that time was Minister of Munitions.

| Photograph of Roosevelt taken in 1913 while he was assistant secretary of the US navy.

In 1920, after overseeing the dismantling of the naval bases in Europe, Roosevelt was nominated as the Democratic vice-presidential candidate, with the party hoping to capitalise on the reputation he had acquired during the war. However, the Republican Warren G. Harding (1865-1923), who campaigned on the theme of a return to normalcy, soundly defeated the Democratic candidate James Cox (1870-1957).

Difficult years and election as governor of New York

After the Democrats' defeat, Roosevelt went back to his law career as the head of a New York law firm. In 1921, while he was staying with his family at his property in Campobello (Canada), he contracted an illness that left his lower body permanently paralysed. He was subsequently diagnosed with poliomyelitis.

ROOSEVELT'S PARALYSIS

Although some doctors predicted that Roosevelt would regain the use of his legs, he never dided. He treated his illness through hydrotherapy at his property in Georgia. Over time, he learned to move around in a wheelchair in private, while in public he relied on orthopaedic braces and canes, and supported himself on the arm of one of his sons or, later on, of one of his advisors.

Recent studies have suggested that Roosevelt's illness was not poliomyelitis but rather Guillain-Barré syndrome, a rare auto-immune disease which attacks the immune system.

Although Roosevelt continued to take an interest in the affairs of the Democratic Party in the years following his paralysis, it was several years before he returned to the political stage. The 1928 gubernatorial and presidential elections were a key stage in his career. Shortly after his re-election as governor of New York in 1930, he developed a social programme to mitigate the effects of the 1929 Wall Street Crash. This included in particular the Temporary Emergency Relief Administration, which provided financial assistance to the unemployed. His re-election made Roosevelt President Herbert Hoover's (1874-1964) most significant rival thanks to the dominant role played by the state of New York in US politics.

THE 32ND PRESIDENT OF THE UNITED STATES OF AMERICA

On 8 November 1932, Roosevelt was elected president of the United States of America. However, as stipulated in the Constitution, he could not be sworn into office before 4 March 1933. During this transitional period, he surrounded himself with a group of intellectuals and worked with them to develop a series of measures designed to halt the crisis and kick-start economic recovery. This group of intellectuals would later be known as his "Brain Trust".

ROOSEVELT'S BRAIN TRUST

Throughout his political career, Roosevelt surrounded himself with trusted advisors. The first to join his team was Louis Howe (1871-1936), whom he met at the beginning of his career. He was subsequently joined by Frances Perkins (1880-1965) and Harry Hopkins (1890-1946), who followed Roosevelt to Washington D.C. He added more academics and intellectuals to his team between his election as president and the official start of his term to form his so-called Brain Trust. These advisors played a crucial role in the development of the New Deal.

The New Deal (1933-1941)

The New Deal refers to Roosevelt's voluntarist, progressive, interventionist economic policy. It began with 15 new emergency laws promulgated during the first 100 days of his presidency in order to halt the crisis. They were followed by wholesale reform of the economic sector, and more specifically by the reorganisation of the banking, financial, agricultural and industrial sectors. This reform used social programmes and large-scale public works initiatives to combat overproduction, destructive competition and unemployment. It also aimed to restore American citizens' buying power and modernise working conditions. Recovery was slow to begin with, and Roosevelt did not hesitate to massively increase public spending in order to reduce unemployment and stimulate consumption. As a result, the USA's public debt doubled.

Roosevelt's war leadership

Although the USA did not openly intervene in European affairs, towards the end of the 1930s it provided military assistance to the continent's democracies. This collaboration intensified when Great Britain was left facing the Axis alone. However, the USA did not officially enter the war until after the Japanese army's attack on the Pearl Harbor naval base on 7 December 1941.

| Photograph of the attack on the Pearl Harbor naval base.

Throughout the conflict, Roosevelt demonstrated impressive leadership capacity and developed his military and strategic abilities. He took firm stances on a number of operations and decisions, such as pushing for the enemy's unconditional surrender. He discussed military and political matters with Winston Churchill and Joseph Stalin in meetings and conferences in Casablanca, Tehran and Yalta. These talks laid the foundations for the Normandy landings and the creation of the United Nations.

| The Yalta Conference, February 1945.

By late March 1945, Roosevelt was suffering from fatigue and worsening health, so he retired to Georgia to recuperate. He died at his home in Warm Springs on 12 April following a brain haemorrhage. His death came just a few months after the beginning of his fourth term as president and less than a month before the Allied victory in Europe, and triggered an outpouring of grief in the USA and around the world.

Roosevelt's funeral procession.

POLITICAL, SOCIAL AND ECONOMIC CONTEXT

AMERICAN POLITICS

From the Great War to the Treaty of Versailles

In the early 1910s, the American political climate was favourable to the Democrats: Woodrow Wilson was elected president in 1912, while the Republican Party was riven by internal divisions.

Wilson's presidency saw the introduction of new progressive legislation, namely the Clayton Antitrust Act of 1914 and the granting of women's suffrage in 1920, but his two terms were marked above all by the First World War. When the conflict broke out in Europe in August 1914, the US government stood firm and asserted its neutrality. This stance was supported by the majority of the American public. Throughout the conflict, US banks lent money to the European powers ($2.3 billion to the Allies and $30 million to Germany).

The USA did not enter the war until 1917. There were a number of reasons behind this decision, such as Germany's policy of targeting both enemy ships and neutral merchant ships (including American ships) with its submarines off the coasts of the British Isles.

| Wilson asking Congress whether the USA should enter the war, 2 April 1917.

At the end of the conflict, Wilson set out a series of diplomatic principles in his Fourteen Points.

The resulting discussions served as a basis for peace negotiations which led to the drawing up of the Treaty of Versailles. Some of his proposals, such as the reduction of armaments, the end of secret diplomacy, populations' right to self-determination and the creation of a League of Nations tasked with peacefully resolving conflicts, were revolutionary for the time.

Wilson's reputation and prestige in Europe continued to grow, and he went to the continent to participate in the peace negotiations in person. However, the esteem in which he was held there was in stark contrast to the situation on the other side of the Atlantic. Following the 1918 legislative elections, the Republicans took control of Congress and opposed the results of Wilson's negotiations. They believed that it was time to return to focusing on domestic affairs (the economic crisis due to inflation between 1919 and 1920, widespread strike action, the fear of Bolsheviks) rather than trying to maintain order around the world as part of the League of Nations. Furthermore, membership of this organisation risked creating conflict with the USA's foreign policy in Latin America.

Republican dominance (1920-1932)

The 1920 presidential election was won by the Republican candidate, and the party remained in power until the early 1930s. The result of this election constituted a rejection of progressive advances, Wilson's foreign policy and the country's membership of the League of Nations.

REPUBLICAN FOREIGN POLICY: UNILATERALISM

During this period, the USA did not completely isolate itself from the rest of the world, but foreign relations no longer played a central role in American politics. The country's foreign policy was therefore not strictly speaking isolationist, but can be better described as unilateralist: foreign policy decisions now only served their own interests.

For example, the Allies' failure to repay the loans they had taken out during the war pushed the USA to intervene in the payment process for the reparations imposed on Germany in the peace treaties, as these reparations would give the Allies the money they needed to repay their debts.

At the same time, in order to maintain peace and ensure balance between their respective navies, Great Britain, France, Italy and the USA signed a series of treaties in the early 1920s. Later on, in 1928, the Kellogg-Briand Pact between France and the USA, which was signed by numerous other countries, tried to strengthen the newly established peace by outlawing war.

As such, the "return to normalcy" promised by Warren G. Harding's campaign triumphed and the country turned inwards and embraced nationalism. However, in many ways Harding was not cut out for the presidency, and preferred playing golf and poker to working on matters of national interest. His government, which was made up of his conservative cronies and some Republicans, made little impact, apart from the introduction of protectionist measures in some sectors of the economy and the development of a socially unequal fiscal policy which reduced taxes for the USA's wealthiest citizens to avoid impeding their business activities. Harding died in 1923, and never addressed the corruption scandals which dogged his administration.

He was succeeded by his vice-president Calvin Coolidge (1872-1933), who governed the country in the interim period before the 1924 presidential elections, which he won. His leadership was scarcely more effective than Harding's, but he enjoyed considerable popularity. Indeed, Coolidge was associated with the country's prosperity, and the Republican Party benefitted from this reputation until the late 1920s. He was an advocate of *laissez-faire* (meaning that the government should not interfere in business, finance and working conditions) and managed to reduce government debt through budgetary savings.

During this decade, Northern and Southern Democrats clashed over crucial issues including immigration, religion and Prohibition. As a result, the party lacked a real leader to challenge the Republicans in presidential elections.

THE ROARING TWENTIES

The period from the end of the First World War in 1918 to the advent of the Great Depression in 1929 is often known as the Roaring Twenties in the USA. This decade was characterised by an economic boom which ensured the country's prosperity and by a range of changes in everyday life, consumer habits and culture.

The economic boom

Between 1919 and 1929, the USA enjoyed impressive economic growth: the country's GNP rose from \$78.9 billion to \$104.4 billion, which was equivalent to an annual growth rate of over 4%. This economic boom was a result of the Second Industrial Revolution, which began in the second half of the 19th century and ushered in the age of mass production. This increase in productivity was made possible by a range of technological advances.

In particular, electricity replaced steam as the primary source of energy in factories. In addition, scientific management (also known as Taylorism) was developed by Frederick Winslow Taylor and sought to break down the production process in order to make each worker more efficient. This marked the beginning of the assembly line.

The biggest advances in production in the 1920s came in the automobile industry. The assembly lines in the Ford factory and the development of the Ford Model T resulted in both a boom in automobile production (from 1.5 million units in 1921 to 4.7 million units in 1929) and lower prices. By the end of the decade, one American in six owned a car. Other sectors, such as radio, aeronautics, steel, oil and film also experienced a significant increase in productivity.

| Employees working on the assembly line in the Ford factory.

The Republican-dominated 1920s saw a wave of acquisitions and mergers, primarily horizontal integrations, whereas the antitrust laws introduced by the previous progressive governments had sought to put an end to these anti-competitive practices. This policy, which was introduced by the Secretary of Commerce and future president Herbert Hoover, allowed sizeable companies, or corporations, to be created by grouping jobs together, and resulted in integrations in the electricity and automobile industries. This in turn saw the emergence of the first holdings and the concept of big business, meaning large-scale activity involving vast sums of money.

However, this economic prosperity did not reach all sectors of the economy, and industries such as coal, shipyards, textiles and agriculture were left out of the overall growth. The situation was particularly grave in the agricultural sector, which was often beset by serious difficulties due to overproduction, price collapses and the lack of governmental measures to resolve crises.

The emergence of the consumer society

As is to be expected, this prosperity went hand in hand with growth in consumption prompted by increased buying power. The average income per person rose from $522 to $716. However, once again this prosperity was unevenly distributed: while businesses' profits increased by 62% between 1923 and 1929, workers' salaries only rose by 26% over the same period. America had an increasing number of millionaires, but there were still major differences in salary between different industries and different states. Although the unemployment rate decreased, the country did not reach full employment. In spite of these disparities, consumption increased across American society and newspaper and radio advertising spread.

THE APPEARANCE OF THE RADIO

Radio sets went on sale for the first time in 1920 in Pittsburgh, Pennsylvania. Ten years later, 14 million American families had one and used it to listen to the news, music, sports broadcasts, political speeches and the results of presidential elections. Roosevelt was the first president to use the radio to directly address the entire American population in his "fireside chats". During these broadcasts, he informed the public about the measures taken by his government, in particular during the economic crises of the 1930s. As he was addressing a large audience, he chose his words carefully to ensure that everyone understood him and restore the population's confidence.

The radio set was not the only invention to revolutionise citizens' daily lives, as the arrival of electricity in towns and cities allowed Americans to acquire telephones, gramophones, refrigerators, vacuum cleaners, radiators, irons, washing machines and other labour-saving appliances. Furthermore, at this time women began enjoying greater freedom and flappers appeared. These women cut their hair short, wore short skirts and danced the Charleston.

The development of industry, the importance placed on business and the growing need for a flourishing services sector resulted in the growth of cities and the development of the railways. By now, most US citizens lived in urban areas which were constantly growing, both horizontally, with the construction of modern, peaceful suburbs on their outskirts and the expansion of medium-sized cities, and horizontally, with the construction of skyscrapers such as the Empire State Building (completed in 1931), which remained the tallest building in the world until the early 1960s. These metropolises became increasingly standardised, and certain types of establishments sprang up throughout urban areas. These included garages and service stations, which attest to the rise of the automobile, and cinemas and stadiums, which marked the beginning of the entertainment era.

Although some leisure establishments had developed before the war, they became far more popular during the 1920s. This can be seen with the success of the film industry in Hollywood, the growing popularity of cinemas (the number of viewers per week rose from 22 million at the start of the 1920s to 29 million, or 80% of the American population, by the end of the decade), and the number of films produced per year (around 700). The music industry was also booming during this period, as record companies innovated with country music and above all with jazz, which became popular during the 1920s.

Greater social conservatism

In the aftermath of the war, a current of conservative values developed alongside the country's growing prosperity and positivity and increasingly relaxed social mores. This current extolled Protestant morality and opposed what its adherents saw as harmful influences in modern society, such as lax morals, Communism, atheism and anything else that did not match their vision of the American ideal.

The Ku Klux Klan (KKK), which had been disbanded in 1870, re-emerged in the South in 1915 before spreading across the country and gaining many new members. The KKK's activity was based on a combination of racism towards the black community and a strain of Americanism that opposed anyone who threatened the country's perceived traditional values, namely Jews, Catholics, Communists and recent immigrants. Intimidation and lynchings became frequent occurrences. The KKK's influence also stretched into politics, tainting both of the main parties and influencing the governance of some states.

Finally, one of the best-known policies of this period was Prohibition, with the 18th Amendment to the Constitution which was passed in 1919 and became law the following year. This was the fruit of a long struggle for moral improvement by the Protestant Church, while progressive movements saw it as a positive step for public health and industrial productivity. Prohibition was co-opted by conservative and extremist movements such as the KKK, which used it to stigmatise foreigners who consumed alcohol, such as the Italians, Irish and Polish. While several states had already banned alcohol, this amendment made the production, sale and transport of drinks stronger than 0.5% a criminal offence. However, consuming alcohol was not in itself a crime. Prohibition divided American society in two, with a sharp contrast between the dry counties in the South and wet counties in the North.

| Detroit police examining the equipment in a clandestine brewery.

The main challenge of Prohibition was not to get the amendment passed, but to enforce it, as regulations and the manpower available varied from one state to another. Furthermore, many of the officials tasked with enforcing Prohibition were deeply corrupt. The American public did not lose their taste for drink, which meant that many clandestine establishments sprang up and poorer citizens distilled their own alcohol, which was often contaminated and carried significant health risks. It was not long before a black market emerged, and bootleggers smuggled alcoholic beverages into the country from Canada, Mexico and the French overseas territory of Saint Pierre and Miquelon. This trade was in the hands of organised criminal gangs whose members often had immigrant roots. One of the most famous gangsters of the period was Al Capone (1899-1947). The amendment was not repealed until 1933, when the country was mired in the Great Depression. From this point onwards, each state was free to take the measures it deemed appropriate to regulate alcohol consumption within its territory.

THE GREAT DEPRESSION

The Republican Herbert Hoover was sworn in as president at the start of 1929. The former Secretary of Commerce was a firm believer in the country's prosperity and campaigned under the slogan "A chicken in every pot and a car in every garage". During his presidency, he tried to further strengthen the economy and took a confident approach. Meanwhile, the Democratic leader claimed that is was possible to get rich by saving $15 per week. US citizens wholeheartedly believed that it was a great time to be alive, and euphoria and prosperity reigned supreme. Only a small handful of intellectuals predicted that it would all come crashing down.

In the 1920s, stock market speculation became something of a craze, with 5.5 million Americans regularly playing the markets. Many people were caught up in the excitement and were convinced that they could get rich quickly and effortlessly thanks to the big profits to be had on the stock exchange on Wall Street. They either used their savings to buy shares or took out bank loans to pay for bonds.

The stock market collapse

Even before the market collapsed, there were signs that the American economy was in poor shape, such as excessive speculation and a lack of guarantees when granting credit to individuals. In September 1929, the stock exchange wavered, before plummeting at the start of October and suffering a crash three weeks later.

STOCK MARKET CRASHES

A stock market crash occurs when stock market values collapse suddenly following a rush of selling orders or the bursting of a speculative bubble. A speculative bubble refers to a disproportionate spike in asset values on the financial markets in relation to the real value of the asset.

The Wall Street Crash took place on 24 October, which went down in history as Black Thursday. Only two thirds of the 19 million shares on the market found buyers. Prices fell so rapidly that the teleprinters could not keep up, so speculators sold their shares without knowing how much they were worth. The following Tuesday, 29 October (known as Black Tuesday), is widely held to be the most catastrophic day and marked the end of the crash. Out of a total of 30 million shares, only 16.5 million were sold, no matter the share price. Even after the crash came to an end, share prices continued to fall for the remainder of the final quarter. Total losses for the year were estimated at $30 billion dollars, or ten times the federal budget.

The crash took American citizens by surprise, as they had been overconfident and had never thought that share prices could fall so rapidly. The crash was followed by the Great Depression, which did not end until the USA entered the Second World War in 1941.

From financial crisis to economic depression

The first casualty of the bursting of the speculative bubble was the world of finance. Lenders demanded cash from their borrowers (speculators and underwriters), but only received share titles whose value had plummeted. Between 1929 and 1932, some 5000 banks and investment firms went bankrupt, which meant that millions of Americans saw their savings wiped out overnight. The financial crisis also had an impact on economic activity as it affected businesses' investments.

The financial crisis therefore triggered a snowball effect which resulted in a full-blown economic crisis. Starting in summer 1929, things were looking bleak across a number of sectors, including the automobile sector and the housing sector. As a result of the Wall Street Crash, these sectors found few buyers, which was a problem as their productivity was based on continued demand and households reduced their consumption once they had already made a purchase. The situation was exacerbated by the unequal distribution of wealth: the purchasing power of a small section of the population was not high enough to sustain the prosperity of the 1920s.

This situation caused a chain reaction: companies had less and less cash to keep their operations running; productivity declined, resulting in lower salaries and layoffs as companies could not afford to pay their employees; this increase in unemployment (there were 15 million unemployed working-age citizens in 1933, up from 4.5 million in 1930) drove down consumption and increased stocks, forcing companies to file for bankruptcy.

The American population was left fearing for its future. Soup kitchens reappeared and families who could not pay their rent were forced onto the street and had their goods seized. They then had no choice but to settle in vacant lots, where they built makeshift shelters out of corrugated metal and cardboard. This gave rise to shanty towns known as Hoovervilles, which appeared all over the country.

| Photograph of a Hooverville in Oregon.

Hoover's policies

Hoover's speech on prosperity when he was sworn in as president in 1929 left a bitter aftertaste in the wake of Black Tuesday. Like most Americans, Hoover was blindsided by the economic crisis and the Great Depression which followed it. Furthermore, he had no intention of stepping in to alleviate the crisis, because he saw federal intervention as an infringement of individual freedom and a hindrance to the work of the local authorities, which should, in his view, be responsible for managing the situation.

Nonetheless, he took steps to restore confidence, as he saw the collapse in confidence as one of the reasons for the crisis. However, in spite of his many promises and statements about recovery, the crisis worsened and the president's credibility was irrevocably tarnished. At the same time, he met with the owners of big businesses in order to encourage them to maintain workers' salaries and keep investing. He gave grants to farmers and implemented a public works programme to create jobs for some of the unemployed workers. He also introduced protectionist measures with a new law on customs tariffs, which ultimately worsened the crisis.

The spread of the crisis

Although the crisis began in the USA, it was not long before it spread across the world and reached Europe, South America and Oceania. Few countries were spared from its effects.

The decline in international trade from 1930 onwards was one of the main reasons the crisis spread to other continents. When the USA reduced its imports, its trading partners saw their income decline, which in turn dented their productivity. These countries then reduced their imports, resulting in a domino effect. The volume of international trade dropped by around 25% and its value fell by around 60% between 1929 and 1932. Other factors which contributed to the spread of the crisis around the world included the implementation of protectionist measures and the devaluation of certain currencies, such as the pound sterling.

Europe, which was in the process of rebuilding itself after the war, was one of the continents that suffered most when the crisis spread. The

Weimar Republic (Germany), which relied on financing from the USA to sustain its economy and reconstruction efforts, was the first country to feel the effects of the recession. It was also the hardest hit, and the untenable consequences of the crisis led indirectly to the outbreak of the Second World War in 1939. In the aftermath of the Wall Street Crash, President Hoover decided to take back the $14 billion dollars that the USA had invested in the Weimar Republic. German banks, which had already been weakened by the collapse of banks in Austria, found themselves short of cash, while ordinary citizens, who had by now lost confidence in the financial institutions, withdrew their meagre savings before their banks went bust. By the start of 1932, the situation had reached catastrophic proportions: exports fell by 25% between 1929 and 1932; industrial production collapsed; more and more businesses went bankrupt; and six million people were now unemployed.

HITLER'S RISE TO POWER

The National Socialist German Workers' Party (NSDAP) was founded in 1920 and led by Adolf Hitler (1889-1945). This far-right party made extensive use of nationalist propaganda and based its programme around the refusal to pay the reparations imposed after the First World War, the rejection of the terms of the Treaty of Versailles, racism and anti-Semitism. Although the NSDAP was only a minority party to begin with, it enjoyed a meteoric rise in popularity in the 1920s as German democracy was weakened by the economic crisis.

The NSDAP won the support of many of the victims of the crisis and a number of industrialists, and scapegoated Communists and Jews for both Germany's defeat in the war and the economic crisis. It also capitalised on the ruling politicians' failure to resolve the country's economic problems. This allowed the party to secure a significant proportion of the vote in the 1932 elections and Hitler to become Chancellor in 1933.

RISING TENSIONS AND THE SECOND WORLD WAR

Nazi Germany's foreign policy was clear: Hitler aimed to unite all the Germanic minorities in a Greater Germany, and then continue to expand into rich territories. To this end, he reintroduced military service and remilitarised the Rhineland. Although these measures both violated the terms of the Treaty of Versailles, Europe's democracies were largely silent.

In October 1936, Nazi Germany began to forge closer links with Mussolini's (1883-1945) fascist Italy, which was already a pariah state within Europe following its invasion of Ethiopia in 1935. This resulted in the Rome-Berlin Axis, and the two countries were joined by Japan a month later. In March 1938, the Wehrmacht (the armed forces of Nazi Germany) occupied Austria and secured *Anchluss*, meaning the union of Austria and Germany. A few months later, Hitler annexed the Sudetenland in Czechoslovakia, which had a considerable German minority, then the entirety of Czechoslovakia, Moravia and Bohemia. The point of no return was reached with the signing of the Molotov-Ribbentrop Pact between Nazi Germany and the USSR, in which the two powers planned to carve up Poland between them. When Germany invaded Poland, Great Britain and France both declared war on the Axis powers. Germany's swift victories in Europe were cause for shock and concern in the USA, particularly after the fall of Paris.

| German soldiers marching in front of the Arc de Triomphe on 14 June 1940.

In spite of a series of Nazi submarine attacks, the USA remained reluctant to intervene directly in European affairs and initially limited its role to supporting Great Britain and the USSR by supplying arms. The *casus belli* came in December 1941, when Japan attacked the Pearl Harbor naval base, the Philippines and Malaysia.

The attack on Pearl Harbor

The bay of Pearl Harbor, which is situated on the island of Oahu, Hawaii, became famous following the surprise attack on it by the Japanese navy and air force. Relations between Washington and Tokyo had been deteriorating for several years prior to the assault as a result of Japanese expansion in Asia. The tipping point was reached in 1940, when the USA and its allies imposed a trade embargo on the Japanese Empire.

The Japanese forces' surprise attack in 1941 targeted the US naval base, and resulted in the sinking of ten warships and the destruction of 188 planes. In the wake of the attack, the US Congress declared war on the Empire of the Rising Sun. This gave rise to virulent anti-Japanese sentiment in the USA, and before long American residents and citizens of Japanese origin were imprisoned in internment camps in the west of the country. Congress did not officially

A few days after the attack, Nazi Germany and fascist Italy also declared war on the USA. Although this meant that the country was fighting on two fronts simultaneously, its priority was the war in Europe.

While preparations were underway for the Normandy landings, US troops carried out operations in Sicily and North Africa and waged bombing campaigns in large German cities to undermine the population's morale. The landings took place on five beaches in Normandy on 6 June 1944, and after this operation France's towns and cities were gradually liberated, culminating with Paris on 24 August. The invasion of western Germany did not begin until February 1945, when Soviet troops were already present in Poland and eastern Germany. The Red Army captured Berlin on 2 June, and Germany surrendered six days later.

In the Pacific Theatre, the US navy did not get the upper hand over its Japanese counterparts until the Battle of Midway in May 1942. The American

marines then had to reconquer the Pacific islands one by one, each of which was ferociously
defended by the Japanese. The advance towards
Japan was slow, and even after the bombardment
and almost total destruction of Tokyo on 23 May
1945 Emperor Hirohito (1901-1989) refused to
capitulate. Japan did not surrender until after
the atomic bombings of Hiroshima on 6 August
and Nagasaki on 9 August on President Truman's
orders. The country's surrender was announced
on 12 August and signed on 2 September.

HIGHLIGHTS

GOVERNORSHIP OF NEW YORK

In 1928, presidential and gubernatorial elections were held in the USA. The Democratic candidate Al Smith (1873-1944) was the governor of New York, the most powerful state in the country, but this was not enough to secure victory over the Republican Herbert Hoover. On the state level, Roosevelt was elected governor of New York and was sworn in on 1 January 1929.

THE IMPORTANCE OF THE STATE OF NEW YORK WITHIN THE USA

During the first half of the 20th century, the state of New York was both the most populous state in the country and the most financially and economically influential state, as it played a dominant role in the industrial, trade and agricultural sectors. Whoever was in charge of the most powerful state in the country therefore had a prominent role on the national stage.

Since the end of the First World War, Al Smith and the Democrats had secured a strong position for themselves in New York politics. During the 1920s, a series of progressive social and fiscal reforms were implemented in the state: indeed, New York was one of the few states to remain relatively untouched by the conservative measures implemented by the ruling Republican Party. After he was sworn in, Roosevelt continued his predecessor's progressive policies while keeping one eye on the next elections. His two main hobby-horses were agricultural problems and the reduction of electricity prices.

However, before long Roosevelt had to face up to the direct effects of the economic crisis, as New York was one of the hardest-hit states: unemployment skyrocketed in both urban areas and the countryside, and social and economic poverty became inescapable. This situation was the driving force behind Roosevelt's entire gubernatorial campaign, which ended in victory in 1931. His campaign was set apart by the projects he planned to implement to combat the Great Depression: in contrast to the approach favoured by Hoover and by Washington, he wanted to continue with progressive policies while simultaneously tackling the unemployment problem.

In 1930, Roosevelt created a committee to fight against layoffs and protect jobs, while one of his advisors, Frances Perkins, was tasked with combatting unemployment. In summer 1931, Roosevelt put forward five measures for the state's struggling localities to implement:

- the creation of the Temporary Emergency Relief Administration (TERA), with a $20 million budget to ensure that food supplies reached the most disadvantaged citizens;
- a 50% increase in income tax paid to the state of New York;
- the financing of public works through three-year loans taken out by local authorities;
- improved working conditions in the public sector (working week limited to five days);
- $500 000 set aside to lift former soldiers out of poverty and get them consuming again.

The TERA, which proposed a new kind of social policy, was central to the measures proposed by Roosevelt, went on to become one of the key elements of the New Deal, and provided inspiration for a number of other states. In addition to an unemployment allowance of $23 per month, enough for a family to eat decently, it also provided jobs. Its budget consistently increased year on year.

PRESIDENCY

The 1932 elections and the start of Roosevelt's presidency

The economic crisis had immediate political consequences: voters wanted change, and they made this clear in the 1930 midterms, when the Republicans lost a large number of seats in Congress. The 1932 presidential elections were a key turning point: they pitted the incumbent President Herbert Hoover against Roosevelt, the Democratic candidate. Roosevelt, who had become very popular during his term as governor thanks to the action he had taken to combat unemployment, promised what he called a "New Deal" to help lift the country out of the crisis. He also promised to end Prohibition. He was a symbol of activism and won over voters thanks to his charisma, whereas the credibility of Hoover and his Republican Party had plummeted.

| Roosevelt campaigning in Warm Springs in 1932.

The Democrats won the elections in December 1932 by a landslide, and Roosevelt became the 32nd president of the United States with a majority of over seven million votes over Hoover. In addition, his party now controlled the legislative branch as it had a majority in both the House of Representatives and the Senate, which was crucial to the new administration's plans to bolster the country's economy.

The New Deal: an interventionist economic programme

The New Deal, which had been designed by Roosevelt's Brain Trust during his presidential campaign, was set into motion the day after he was sworn in, when he summoned Congress for an exceptional session. The first phase of the plan lasted from 1933 to 1935, and during the first three months of Roosevelt's term, legislators passed some 15 laws to ameliorate the dire economic situation. As such, Roosevelt used his first 100 days in office to lay the foundations of the New Deal and demonstrate the government's willingness to intervene in the economy.

The first measure involved the financial sector. On 6 March 1933, the government closed all banks in order to restore some order to the chaotic banking system, boost confidence and halt the flow of gold out of the country. On 9 March, the president signed the Emergency Banking Relief Act, which permitted all solvent banks to reopen the following day and placed them under the control of the Federal Reserve. Other measures were subsequently implemented to further strengthen the sector, such as the introduction of a distinction between deposit banks and merchant banks. In January 1934, in response to recent inflation, the dollar was devalued, which improved the situation.

The Agricultural Adjustment Act (AAA), which was passed in May 1933, marked the government's first intervention in the agricultural sector. Its purpose was to boost prices following a decrease in production and in the area of land cultivated, and it involved paying farmers to make up for this shortfall.

At the same time, the National Industrial Recovery Act (NIRA) was passed in June 1933 and aimed to tackle problems in the industrial sector. It promoted fair competition between businesses to avoid bankruptcies, introduced price controls and proposed a code of conduct for companies which imposed better working conditions (minimum wages and maximum working hours) and established a trade union presence. All businesses which subscribed to this code of conduct affixed the Blue Eagle (the symbol of NIRA) with the slogan "We do our part" to their products.

| Photograph of a woman putting the campaign poster in the window of her restaurant, around 1934.

In May 1933, Congress created the Tennessee Valley Authority (TVA), which set out a vast planning and improvement programme for the five states around Tennessee to be carried out between 1933 and 1939. This innovative project required a vast workforce to construct some 20 dams, which would double the country's electricity production, enable navigation and trade on the river, and promote industrialisation in the region.

To fight unemployment without increasing government spending, the administration created the Civilian Conservation Corps (CCC) on 31 March 1993. The programme provided environmental conservation work for half a million unemployed 18-25-year-olds between 1933 and 1942.

The other major project championed by Congress in May 1933 sought to transpose New York's TERA to the federal level under the name Federal Emergency Relief Administration (FERA). Harry Hopkins was placed in charge of the new organisation. It had a budget of $500 million and provided financial support that states and local communities could use to offer benefits for vulnerable citizens and create jobs through public works projects. The FERA ended up competing with the Public Works Administration (PWA), which was created by the NIRA and headed by the Secretary of the Interior Harold Ickes (1874-1952). Consequently, the Civil Works Administration (CWA) was created in November

1933 and entrusted to Harry Hopkins. This body helped the unemployed directly by creating jobs: it employed a total of over four million people, who built and repaired thousands of miles of roads, schools, stadiums and other infrastructure.

In mid-1934, the first phase of the New Deal came to an end and the situation gradually improved. No major new laws were passed and some programmes were halted. These included the CWA, which was suspected of corruption in spring 1934, and the NIRA (discontinued in 1935) and the AAA (discontinued in 1936), which were ruled unconstitutional by the Supreme Court. A number of movements opposed the New Deal, and the former president labelled its measures fascistic and claimed that the Brain Trust was under the sway of Communism. Nonetheless, the government remained keenly aware of the need to pursue its reforms.

After some of the New Deal's programmes were halted, the government needed to find new solutions to combat the crisis. These were developed during the second phase of the plan, which stretched from 1935 to 1938. The progressive reforms introduced in the early days of the New Deal were no longer enough, so the government adopted further measures which it described as liberal but can be better classified as left-wing.

In April 1935, the Works Public Administration (WPA) was created to replace the CWA, which had been dissolved a few months previously. It worked in a similar way, and was also headed by Harry Hopkins, but was larger in scope: it had more resources at its disposal and created work for eight million people in the public works, construction and culture sectors. At the same time, Congress passed the National Labor Relations Act, which replaced the provisions of the now-repealed NIRA and ensured the independence of trade unions, in spite of vehement opposition.

Significant social progress was also made in this period, as unemployment benefits and retirement allowances were granted to citizens who had already worked. Under the impetus of the Secretary of the Treasury and the Chair of the Federal Reserve, Congress voted for fiscal reform in favour of greater social justice and an increase in the powers of the Federal Reserve to facilitate the financing of government spending.

The following year, the Supreme Court attacked the provisions set out in the New Deal and ruled the AAA unconstitutional. In order to pursue this measure, the government no longer paid farmers to reduce the area they cultivated, but rather to leave some land fallow. In spite of Republican attacks which painted him as a virtual Communist, Roosevelt secured a second term as president in November 1936. After his re-election, he waged a crusade against the Supreme Court, which was constantly working to repeal some of the New Deal's measures. Specifically, he adjusted the number of justices in the country's courts and nominated judges who supported his liberal policies to the Supreme Court. This legal battle was a major issue for most of 1937, and the economic situation, which seemed to be improving, was left to one side for a time.

Given that the situation was improving and the Republicans were putting pressure on the government, it was forced to reduce its spending. The WPA's budget was cut, leaving more than a million workers unemployed, and decisions made by the Federal Reserve raised the interest on credit. Before long, businesses invested less and prices fell, plunging the country into another unexpected economic crisis. By spring 1938, the USA's unemployment rate once again stood at 20%. Perkins and Marriner Stoddard Eccles (1890-1977), the chairman of the Federal Reserve, eventually realised that this relapse was due to the cuts made to reduce the budgetary deficit.

KEYNES'S ECONOMIC THEORIES

In 1936, *The General Theory of Employment, Interest and Money* by the British economist John Maynard Keynes (1883-1946) was published. The book focused on the budget balance: whereas governments at this time sought to balance their income and expenses, Keynes advocated budgetary im-balance. According to him, injecting money into the economy would create jobs, which would in turn increase the population's buying power and kick-start consumption.

Keynes's theories were growing in credibility, and Roosevelt was eventually won over and decided to stop making balancing the budget a priority.

The government then increased its spending, in particular by allocating sizeable budgets to the WPA and the PWA, in order to boost consumption. Economic recovery began quickly, but the unemployment rate remained high: in 1939, nine million people were unemployed. The unemployment rate did not decrease significantly until the following year, when the USA began producing arms, first for Great Britain and then for itself. By 1941, the number of unemployed workers had fallen to 5.5 million.

The Second World War

From 1936 onwards, foreign affairs played an increasingly important role in US politics, although the country did not abandon its policy of non-intervention in international matters. Nonetheless, a shift in policy occurred in 1939, when an amendment was added to the Neutrality Act. This law, which was introduced in 1935, prevented the USA from sending arms or granting loans to countries at war. The first shift occurred in 1937 with the Cash and Carry clause, which allowed warring countries to purchase products and transport them from the USA. In

1939, this clause was expanded to cover weapons, thus allowing France and Great Britain to acquire military supplies.

The USA's support of the countries at war against totalitarian powers intensified after the French defeat in June 1940. Roosevelt did everything he could to support Great Britain, which was now facing Nazi Germany alone. In this turbulent context, he was re-elected for a third term in November 1940. Starting in December of that year, the USA began collaborating more closely with Great Britain and Roosevelt forged a closer relationship with Winston Churchill, who had become prime minister in May 1940. Thanks to the Lend-Lease policy, the USA supplied military material and financial support to Great Britain and, from June 1941 onwards, the USSR.

| Roosevelt and Churchill in 1944.

The production of war material, initially for the Allies and then to prepare for the USA's own entry into the war, became a priority for the country and proved an effective means of combatting unemployment and stimulating economic recovery. The successive armament projects during the conflict produced over 171 000 planes, 90 000 tanks, 1200 ships, 320 000 artillery pieces, four million tonnes of munitions and 15 million firearms.

In August 1941, before the USA's entry into the

war, Roosevelt met Churchill off the coast of Newfoundland, Canada. This meeting strengthened the bond between the two nations and resulted in the Atlantic Charter, which planned for the creation of a new League of Nations, among other points. This meant that the USA was no longer totally neutral in the conflict, although Roosevelt had promised during his re-election campaign that no American soldiers would be sent to fight in Europe. However, this all changed when the Pearl Harbor naval base was attacked in December 1941.

| Roosevelt signing the declaration of war against Japan, 8 December 1941.

After this attack, Congress granted Roosevelt emergency powers which allowed him to make decisions based on the country's economic, strategic and military needs. Although his strategic abilities were relatively limited, Roosevelt set out and advocated for his plans at a series of Allied conferences, during which he regularly met with Churchill, Stalin and other Allied heads of state.

The Second Moscow Conference in August 1942 planned the North Africa Campaign to halt the advance of Nazi Germany's Afrika Korps, which Roosevelt saw as vitally important. He therefore sent troops to Europe, and they achieved some victories in North Africa. In January 1943, the Casablanca Conference prepared further decisive measures and operations. At this conference, Roosevelt pushed for the unconditional surrender of the Axis nations, whereas Churchill favoured a less exacting approach. The conference's objectives also included preparing for the landing in Europe and planning the Italian campaign, which led to the fall of Mussolini. A few months later, the Cairo Conference took place and was attended by Roosevelt, Churchill and Chiang Kai-shek (1887-1975), the leader of the Republic of China. During the conference, decisions were made about postwar Asia and the fate of Japan, such as the dispossession of the islands and territories it was occupying. The Tehran Conference, which took place a few days later, brought the "Big Three" Allied leaders (Roosevelt, Churchill and Stalin) together for the first time and aimed to prepare for the landing of the Allied forces. While Churchill thought that the operation should take place in the Balkans, Roosevelt wanted to land on the French coast. He was supported by Stalin, so the leaders began preparing for the Normandy landings, which were planned for spring 1944.

In February 1945, a few months after the end of the conflict, Stalin, Churchill and Roosevelt met again to plan what would happen to Germany and Japan after the end of the war. The Red Army was now only a few dozen miles from Berlin, which put Stalin in a strong position during the negotiations. The main resolutions of the Yalta Conference concerned the USSR's entry into the war against Japan after the defeat of Germany, the destruction of Nazism and the Germany army, the division of Germany amongst the three winners, the borders of certain European countries, and the creation of the United Nations

(UN). The UN, which would be headed by the four winners of the Second World War (the USSR, the USA, Great Britain and China), would be tasked with ensuring peace and governing international relations. For Roosevelt, the creation of the UN and Soviet support against Japan were so important that he did not even try to negotiate when Stalin laid out his territorial demands.

IMPACT

THE CREATION OF THE UN

Following the failure of the League of Nations, which proved incapable of preventing the Second World War, it was essential to find another solution. The creation of the UN was one of Roosevelt's most cherished projects, and he had been campaigning for it as early as 1920, when he was the vice-presidential candidate in the American elections.

At the start of the conflict, he began working towards the creation of an international body that would serve to ensure peace and resolve international problems. He then tried to rally support for his project when he met major world leaders at Allied conferences. This momentum could have been lost after Roosevelt's death, but fortunately his successor Harry S. Truman shared his outlook. This, along with the fact that, unlike Wilson, Truman enjoyed the support of Congress, meant that he could pursue the project.

On 25 April 1945, less than a month after Roosevelt's death, 50 countries that had fought against the Axis came together in San Francisco to lay the foundations for the United Nations. After two months of intense negotiations between the different delegations, the Charter of the United Nations was drawn up. Nonetheless, the decisions made at earlier conferences, such as the Yalta Conference, were still respected.

It was decided that the Security Council would comprise 11 members, five of which would be permanent (the USA, the USSR, Great Britain, China and France). Decisions would require the support of seven members, but each of the five permanent members would have the right to veto.

THE START OF THE COLD WAR AND THE USA'S INTERVENTIONIST POLICY

Relations between the Allies began to falter before the Second World War was over. Two opposing ideological blocs emerged, one dominated by the USA, the other by the USSR. The breakdown of trust between the Allies can be attributed to several geopolitical issues.

The Potsdam Conference (July-August 1945) decided that Germany's borders should be restored to their 1937 positions, before the first Nazi conquests. The country was then divided into four zones of influence, one each for the USSR, the USA, Great Britain and France. Berlin was divided in the same way. Before long, tensions emerged between the zones controlled by the two blocs, resulting in the creation of the Federal Republic of Germany and the German Democratic Republic in 1949.

After the Nazis were driven out of Eastern Europe, the region was occupied by the Red Army, which worried the Allies and constituted the second bone of contention between the two blocs. Poland, Hungary, Bulgaria, Romania and Czechoslovakia were now under Soviet influence, and although pro-Soviet Communist movements in these countries had initially shared power with other parties, these coalitions did not last, and Communist parties took power between 1945 and 1947. The extension of the Soviet sphere of influence in Europe and the establishment of a buffer zone to protect the USSR's borders worried Western leaders. The standoff between the two blocs was clearly illustrated by the famous Iron Curtain metaphor.

The growing tensions between the two blocs led the American president to develop the Truman Doctrine, which aimed to provide the democracies of Western Europe with financial support for their postwar reconstruction and food supplies to prevent famine. This doctrine was put into practice with the Marshall Plan, which aimed to limit the growth of Communist parties in order to consolidate political alliances and ensure a solvent market for US businesses in Europe. The second part of the plan involved sending financial aid to countries that were under pressure from the USSR, such as Greece and Turkey. The British and American leaders believed that the resistance of these two countries was essential in order to prevent Soviet influence from reaching the Middle East and the USSR from getting its hands on the region's oil reserves.

Other incidents, such as the Czech coup in February 1948 and the Berlin Blockade from June 1948 to May 1949, precipitated a definitive shift in American foreign policy. The pressing need for a defensive alliance resulted in the creation of NATO (North Atlantic Treaty Organisation) in April 1949. By this time, the Cold War was well and truly underway.

A THRIVING ECONOMIC AND SOCIAL CLIMATE

By the end of the war, the economic depression of the 1930s was nothing more than a distant memory. The production needed for military operations lifted the American economy out of the doldrums and created jobs, and by 1945 the USA had the largest economy in the world. Some sectors, such as agriculture, prospered during the war. Industrial production after the war was characterised by technological innovations such as nylon and plastic materials and by the recovery of sectors created in the 1920s.

Furthermore, Truman continued with some of Roosevelt's projects. In particular, he developed programmes which aimed to ensure full employment, increase the minimum wage, improve the social security system, and so on. He also had to oversee the transition from a war economy to a peacetime economy and manage the challenge of demobilisation. The number of soldiers dropped from 12 million to three million between 1945 and 1946. To facilitate their reintegration into society, the federal government committed to finding them work and passed the G.I. Bill in June 1944, which set out a number of provisions and financial support mechanisms for returning soldiers.

THE BEGINNING OF A GOLDEN AGE FOR THE DEMOCRATS AND THE STRENGTHENING OF THE PRESIDENCY

Roosevelt's election in 1932 was a major victory for the Democratic Party, which had been out of power for over 20 years. He was elected four times, a record that cannot be beaten since the 22nd Amendment to the Constitution (adopted in 1947 and ratified by Congress in 1951) limits the number of presidential terms to two.

Roosevelt, who was nicknamed "the boss" by those who worked with him, modernised the presidency. He strengthened the role of the president by creating the White House Staff in 1939, a body of advisors who help the president and his cabinet to make decisions. Roosevelt also increased the power of certain government agencies, and Truman followed the same path during his presidency.

During his four terms as president, Roosevelt lifted his country out of the two most serious crises of the 20th century: the Great Depression in the 1930s and the Second World War. The USA emerged stronger from the conflict and became one of two global superpowers, with a dominant role on the international stage.

SUMMARY

1882
30 Jan.: Birth of Franklin Roosevelt

1910
Beginning of Roosevelt's political career

1911-1912
Roosevelt is senator for the state of New York

1913-1921
Roosevelt is assistant secretary of the US navy

1914-1918
First World War

1920
Roosevelt is the Democratic Party's vice-presidential candidate

1921
Roosevelt contracts poliomyelitis and is forced to put his career on hold

1928
Roosevelt is elected governor of the state of New York

1932

8 Nov.: **Roosevelt is elected president of the United States**

1933

Launch of the New Deal

4 Mar.: Roosevelt is sworn in as president

6 Mar.: All America's banks are closed

1939

The Second World War breaks out

1941

7 Dec.: Attack on Pearl Harbor

8 Dec.: **Roosevelt signs the declaration of war against Japan**

1945

Feb.: Yalta Conference

12 Apr.: Death of Roosevelt

25 Apr.: Inaugural session of the UN

7 May: The Germany army surrenders

2 Sept.: Japan surrenders

- Franklin Delano Roosevelt was born on 30 January 1882 in Hyde Park to an affluent upper-class family. His early education was carried out by governesses, and he continued his schooling in prestigious establishments such as Groton School, Harvard University and Columbia University Law School.
- He joined the Democratic Party in 1910 and was elected senator for the state of New York the following year.
- In 1913, he was appointed assistant secretary of the US navy while Woodrow Wilson was president. He rose to prominence thanks to his role during the First World War, and was chosen as his party's vice-presidential candidate for the 1920 elections.
- In 1921, an illness left his lower body paralysed and forced him to temporarily take a step back from politics. The effects of this illness lasted for the rest of his life. He relied on a wheelchair, canes and leg braces to move around, and often leaned on one of his sons or advisors when he had to stand up.
- Between 1928 and 1932, he served as governor of the state of New York and had to deal with the serious economic problems resulting

from the 1929 Wall Street Crash. One of his most important acts was the creation of the Temporary Emergency Relief Administration (TERA) to combat unemployment.

- In November 1932, he was elected president of the United States. He stayed in power for 12 years and remains the only American president to have been elected four times.

- He implemented a voluntarist, interventionist, progressive economic policy known as the New Deal to combat the Great Depression. Initially, the measures introduced aimed to halt the crisis and reorganise the sectors affected. Later on, the project focused on combatting unemployment through a range of programmes that were largely financed by the federal government.

- After the attack on the Pearl Harbor naval base by the Japanese Empire, he officially brought the USA into the Second World War. During this period, he met a number of Allied leaders and planned campaigns against Nazi Germany. The most notable results of these meetings include the war material supplied to Great Britain and the USSR, the decision to push for the unconditional surrender of the enemy, the

Normandy landings and the creation of the UN, the groundwork for which was laid at the Yalta Conference in 1945.

- He died on 12 April 1945 at his home in Warm Springs, Georgia, just days before the official creation of the UN and a few months before the surrender of Germany and Japan.

We want to hear from you!
Leave a comment on your online library
and share your favourite books on social media!

FIND OUT MORE

BIBLIOGRAPHY

- Kaspi, A. (2014) *Les Américains : Naissance et essor des États-Unis (1607-1954).* Volume 1. Paris: Points.

- Kaspi, A. (2014) *Les Américains : Les États-Unis de 1945 à nos jours.* Volume 2. Paris: Points.

- Kaspi, A. (2012) *Franklin D. Roosevelt.* Paris: Librairie Arthème.

- Kaspi, A. (1988) *Franklin D. Roosevelt.* Paris: Fayard.

- Portes, J. (2013) *Histoire des États-Unis de 1776 à nos jours.* Paris: Armand Colin.

- Robert, F. (2013) *Les années Roosevelt (1932-1945) : entre New Deal et « Home Front ».* Paris: Ellipses Éditions.

ADDITIONAL SOURCES

- Dallek, R. (2017) *Franklin D. Roosevelt: A Political Life.* London: Penguin.

- Daniels, R. (2016) *Franklin D. Roosevelt: The War Years, 1939-1945.* Chicago: University of Illinois Press.

- Daniels, R. (2015) *Franklin D. Roosevelt: Road to the New Deal, 1882-1939*. Chicago: University of Illinois Press.

ICONOGRAPHIC SOURCES

- Photograph of Roosevelt at Groton School at the age of 18. Royalty-free reproduction picture.

- Photograph of Roosevelt taken in 1913 while he was assistant secretary of the US navy. Royalty-free reproduction picture.

- Photograph of the attack on the Pearl Harbor naval base. Royalty-free reproduction picture.

- The Yalta Conference. © US Army Signal Corps.

- Roosevelt's funeral procession. Royalty-free reproduction picture.

- Wilson asking Congress whether the USA should enter the war, 2 April 1917. © Library of Congress.

- Employees working on the assembly line in the Ford factory. Royalty-free reproduction picture.

- Detroit police examining the equipment in a clandestine brewery. Royalty-free reproduction picture.

- Photograph of a Hooverville in Oregon. Royalty-free reproduction picture.

- German soldiers marching in front of the Arc de

Triomphe on 14 June 1940. © Bundesarchiv.

- Roosevelt campaigning in Warm Springs in 1932. © Presidential Library & Museum.

- Photograph of a woman putting the campaign poster in the window of her restaurant, around 1934. © National Archives and Records Administration.

- Roosevelt and Churchill in 1944. © National Archives and Records Administration.

- Roosevelt signing the declaration of war against Japan, 8 December 1941. © Abbie Rowe.

DOCUMENTARIES

- *1929.* (2009) [Documentary]. William Karel. Dir. France: Roche Productions.

- *Apocalypse: Second World War.* (2009) [TV miniseries documentary]. France: CC&C, Établissement de Communication et de Production Audiovisuelle de la Défense, NHK.